"As a pastor, I get asked lots of questions. I'm approached by unbelievers seeking to understand the gospel, new believers unsure about next steps, and maturing believers wanting help answering questions from their Christian family, friends, neighbors, or coworkers. It's in these moments that I wish I had a book to give them that was brief, answered their questions, and pointed them in the right direction for further study. Church Questions is a series that provides just that. Each booklet tackles one question in a biblical, brief, and practical manner. The series may be called Church Questions, but it could be called 'Church Answers.' I intend to pick these up by the dozens and give them away regularly. You should too."

Juan R. Sanchez, Senior Pastor, High Pointe Baptist Church, Austin, Texas

Why
Should I
Be Baptized?

Church Questions

Why
Should I
Be Baptized?

Bobby Jamieson

CROSSWAY

WHEATON, ILLINOIS

Why Should I Be Baptized?

Copyright © 2020 by 9Marks

Published by Crossway
        1300 Crescent Street
        Wheaton, Illinois 60187

Cover design: Jordan Singer

First printing 2020

Printed in the United States of America

Trade paperback ISBN: 978-1-4335-7030-8
ePub ISBN: 978-1-4335-7033-9
PDF ISBN: 978-1-4335-7030-8
Mobipocket ISBN: 978-1-4335-7032-2

Library of Congress Cataloging-in-Publication Data

Names: Jamieson, Bobby, 1986- author.
Title: Why should I be baptized? / Bobby Jamieson.
Description: Wheaton, Illinois : Crossway, [2020] |
Series: Church questions | Includes bibliographical references and index.
Identifiers: LCCN 2020003323 (print) | LCCN 2020003324 (ebook) | ISBN 9781433570308 (trade paperback) | ISBN 9781433570308 (pdf) | ISBN 9781433570322 (mobi) | ISBN 9781433570339 (epub)
Subjects: LCSH: Baptism. | Baptism—Biblical teaching. |Salvation—Baptists.
Classification: LCC BV811.3 .J36 2020 (print) | LCC BV811.3 (ebook) | DDC 234/.161—dc23
LC record available at https://lccn.loc.gov/2020003323
LC ebook record available at https://lccn.loc.gov/2020003324

Crossway is a publishing ministry of Good News Publishers.

BP		31	30	29	28	27	26	25	24	23	22	21
14	13	12	11	10	9	8	7	6	5	4	3	2

See, here is water! What prevents
me from being baptized?

Acts 8:36

As you have probably discovered from the title, the goal of this booklet is to persuade you to be baptized. But this booklet's aim applies to you only if two other "ifs" also apply: (1) *if* you have repented of your sins and trusted in Christ for salvation, and (2) *if* you have not yet been baptized as a believer in Christ.

Let's talk about that first "if."

The first recorded words of Jesus's public ministry are, "The time is fulfilled, and the kingdom of God is at hand; repent and believe in the gospel" (Mark 1:15). To repent is to turn, to turn away from sin and turn toward God (Matt. 3:8; Acts 20:21). To repent is to reverse course, to perform an about-face. To repent is to recognize God's authority over you and the ways that you have rejected and resisted his authority. To repent is to acknowledge that you have tried to live as your own master in the past and to embrace Jesus Christ as your Lord, now and forever.

This radical 180-degree turn of repentance is only possible as an act of faith. Faith in whom? Faith in what? Faith in Christ as he offers himself to you in the gospel. Jesus came to earth not just to teach and to heal but also to die and to triumph over death. As sinners, we all deserve God's eternal retribution. This judgment is ultimately what Jesus came to save us from. This judgment is what he endured on the cross (Rom. 3:21–26). This judgment is what he banished from the lives all who believe through his rising from the dead (Rom. 4:25). The way you receive this gracious gift is simply by turning away from sin and trusting Christ.

So have you turned from sin and trusted in Christ?

If not, repent and believe today. Right now. Confess to God that you have spurned him and sinned against him. Place your trust in Christ to save you and confess your faith to God in prayer. This gospel, the good news Jesus came to proclaim and accomplish, is the most important news you can ever hear. Trusting Christ as he is offered to you in the gospel is the most important decision you can ever make.

Baptism, the subject of this booklet, is far less important than the gospel. Nevertheless, baptism is important precisely because baptism is about the gospel. Baptism is attached to the gospel and depicts the gospel. If the gospel is important to you, baptism should be too—important enough for you to do it.

Now, let's briefly talk about that second "if." Have you been baptized as a believer? Perhaps you genuinely believe the gospel now, but are uncertain if you truly trusted Christ at the time you were baptized. *Was I really trusting in Christ when grandpa baptized me at age 8?* Ultimately, I cannot tell you what to do. That's between you and the Lord. If you sincerely believed what you understood at the time about Christ's death and resurrection and the forgiveness of sin, then you may not need to do anything further. However, if you become convinced that you were not born again at the time when you were baptized, then you still need to be baptized. Not "re-baptized," but simply baptized. The bottom line is pray, ask God for wisdom, and then press ahead rejoicing that salvation comes through faith alone in Christ alone.

With these foundations laid, let's talk about baptism. You could think of this booklet as a brief dialogue about baptism. In the first section, we ask, "Why should I get baptized?" In the second section, we address some of the most common objections to getting baptized: "I don't want to get baptized because . . ." And finally, the last section deals with the question, "What should I do now?"

Let's get started.

Why Should I Get Baptized?

Why should you get baptized? Let me give you three reasons. My hope in laying out these reasons is that you will find them not only persuasive but also inviting and compelling. As we'll see, Christ not only commands believers to get baptized, baptism is also a gift he graciously gives for our benefit and blessing.

Here then are three reasons to get baptized: (1) to obey Christ's command, (2) to publicly profess faith in Christ, and (3) to formally commit yourself to Christ and his people.

1. To Obey Christ's Command

Why should you get baptized? To obey Christ's command. Which command? The one he gives us in Matthew 28:19. Let's look at this verse in context:

> And Jesus came and said to them, "All authority in heaven and on earth has been given to me. Go therefore and make disciples of all nations, baptizing them in the name of the Father and of the Son and of the Holy Spirit, teaching them to observe all that I have commanded you. And behold, I am with you always, to the end of the age." (Matt. 28:18–20)

Here Jesus addressed his eleven disciples shortly after he died for our sins and rose from the dead. He had accomplished salvation, and now he charged his disciples to proclaim news of this salvation to every nation on the earth. In verse 18, we learn that as a result of his saving death and resurrection, Jesus possesses "all authority in heaven and on earth." He is the supreme ruler of the universe, the sovereign of sovereigns.

Jesus then gave his disciples—and by implication all believers—one main command: "Make disciples" (v. 19). Jesus commanded his disciples to make disciples. He requires his followers, then and now, to summon others to follow him. He then gave three supporting instructions that show us how to "make disciples." First, we need to *go*. We need to go to where the nations are, whether that means crossing the street, crossing town, or crossing an ocean. Second, we baptize those who follow Christ. And finally, he tells us to instruct new disciples to obey every one of his commands. To become Jesus's follower is to give your whole life to trusting Jesus, following

Jesus, learning and obeying Jesus's teaching, and following Jesus's example.

So according to Jesus, we "make disciples" by baptizing true believers and teaching them to obey all that Jesus commanded. The order is important: make disciples, baptize, teach.

Are you a disciple of Jesus? Then you need to show it by baptism—that's what Jesus said. Jesus wants those who have trusted him as Savior and submitted to him as Lord to get baptized. As you can see, then, baptism publicly identifies someone as a disciple of Jesus. Baptism formally and publicly enrolls a disciple in the school of Christ.

God *marks* his people by baptism. By getting baptized, we are essentially putting on a jersey that says "Team Jesus"—we're playing by his rules and following his commands. By following Jesus's command to get baptized, we're saying we're committed to do *all* that he commanded.

Now, what exactly does Jesus mean when he says "baptize"? Here is a definition of baptism I offered in another short book, called *Understanding Baptism*:

> Baptism is a church's act of affirming and portraying a believer's union with Christ by immersing him or her in water, and a believer's act of publicly committing him or herself to Christ and his people, thereby uniting a believer to the church and marking off him or her from the world.[1]

Now that's a bit of a mouthful. More simply, baptism is a believer's act of publicly committing him or herself to Christ and his people by being immersed in water.

We have already seen from Jesus's teaching in Matthew 28:19 that baptism is how someone publicly commits to follow Christ. And we'll see biblical support for much of this definition in the next two sections. Here we can simply note that baptism should be performed by immersion. The Greek word *baptizō*, on which our word "baptize" is based, means to dip or plunge something completely into a liquid. New Testament examples of baptism imply that it was done by immersion (John 3:23; Acts 8:38–39), and immersion best fits the imagery of union with Christ in his burial and resurrection, which we will consider in the next section (Rom. 6:1–4).

To summarize Jesus's teaching in Matthew 28:19, we can say that baptism is the first item on Jesus's list of "Everything I Have Commanded You." Why should you get baptized? Because if you consider yourself a follower of Jesus, then, after repenting and believing (Mark 1:15), the first formal, public act of following that Jesus requires of you is baptism. The Christian life is more than following commands, but it certainly isn't less. So after the command to repent and believe, here's your first "to-do" from Jesus. All you have to do is declare your faith and lean back.

2. To Publicly Profess Faith in Him

A second reason why you should get baptized is to publicly profess your faith in Jesus. We've seen that this element of baptism is implicit in Matthew 28:19. It's more explicit in a few other places in Scripture.

For example, when those who heard Peter preach on Pentecost were convicted of their sin, they asked him what to do, and he urged them to repent and be baptized (Acts 2:37–38). And then we read, "So those who received his word were baptized, and there were added that day about three thousand souls" (v. 41). Receiving the word and being baptized went hand in hand. All those who embraced the gospel were baptized, and only those who embraced the gospel were baptized. Baptism was how those at Pentecost publicly proclaimed their embrace of Christ, the crucified and resurrected Messiah. And baptism is how you can and should openly declare that you trust in Christ.

Similarly, consider Paul's teaching in Colossians 2:11–12:

> In him also you were circumcised with a circumcision made without hands, by putting off the body of the flesh, by the circumcision of Christ, having been buried with him in baptism, in which you were also raised with him through faith in the

powerful working of God, who raised him from the dead.

Note how baptism and faith go hand in hand. Addressing a congregation of baptized Christians, Paul says that they were buried and raised with Christ in baptism. He even uses baptism as a shorthand to refer to the whole event of their conversion.

He does this because baptism is a visible, tangible, public, dramatic expression of faith in Christ. It's obvious, memorable, datable. You get soaked, and everyone present sees you disappear under the water and reappear up out of the water. That's why Paul singles out baptism as a sign of conversion. But he doesn't just refer to baptism. He says, "in which you were also raised with him *through faith*" (v. 12). Paul assumes that faith was present at the time of baptism, because faith was the reason for baptism. Faith in the resurrection power of God is why those Christians presented themselves for baptism. And publicly expressing that same faith is why you should be baptized too.

Why is it a good thing to publicly declare your faith in Christ? We've already seen that Christ commands it. In addition, declaring your faith in Christ is good for your faith. Declaring your faith will deepen your faith. Confessing your faith will confirm your faith. Sharing your faith will strengthen your faith.

Not only that, but baptism shows us the shape of the whole Christian life. If you're a Christian, you can't just declare your faith once in baptism and then go radio silent about Jesus for the rest of your life. Instead, openly declaring your faith in Christ should be part of the regular fabric of your life from now on. One of the first things people learn about you should be that you're a Christian. That Christ is your Savior should be what you're most excited to tell people. Further, Jesus himself warns that faith that stays a secret is no faith at all. "So everyone who acknowledges me before men, I also will acknowledge before my Father who is in heaven, but whoever denies me before men, I also will deny before my Father who is in heaven" (Matt. 10:32–33).

3. To Commit to Christ's People

We've seen that in baptism you commit to Christ. Now we will see that in baptism you commit to Christ's people. As we've already seen, on the day of Pentecost, those who received the word were baptized and *added to the church* (Acts 2:41). All those who received Christ that day were received by the church. And the way the church received them was by baptizing them. In baptism, you step out of the world and into the church. In baptism, you declare your loyalty to Christ. In baptism, you enlist in Christ's company. Your commitment to Christ's people follows logically, necessarily, and immediately from your commitment to Christ.

The commitment that those who were baptized on Pentecost made with the church was no mere ticking of a box. Instead, this new commitment to Christ's people fundamentally altered the fabric of their lives. We read in the following verses that the whole church in Jerusalem, including these three thousand who joined the church by baptism on Pentecost, devoted themselves to the apostles' teaching, to fellowship, to breaking bread, and to praying together (v. 42). They shared their lives and their possessions (v. 44). They even sold off property in order to give the proceeds to believers in need (v. 45). They prayed and ate together daily (v. 46). The fruit of their commitment to one another was a rich, inviting communion with one another, a communion that inspired awe in outsiders (v. 43). And the means by which they committed to one another was baptism. In baptism those believers bound themselves to Christ and to each other. In other words, in baptism you commit to Christ's people.

We also see that baptism commits a Christian to Christ's people in 1 Corinthians 12:13. Paul writes, "For in one Spirit we were all baptized into one body—Jews or Greeks, slaves or free—and all were made to drink of one Spirit." Is Paul referring to baptism in water or baptism by the Spirit? I would suggest that Paul has both in mind. Christians are reborn and united with Christ and his body by the work of the Spirit, and our baptism in water signifies that baptism by the Spirit.

Some people question whether being "baptized into one body" refers to the universal church or the local church. Here again I would suggest that the former implies the latter. Elsewhere, Paul occasionally uses the concept of the "body" of Christ to describe all believers at all times in all places (see Eph. 1:22–23). But, in the following verses in 1 Corinthians, Paul focuses on a local church. Only in a local church can one member wrongly say to another, "I don't need you" (1 Cor. 12:21). Only in a local church can members honor the less-honored (vv. 23–24). Only in a local church can all suffer together, and all rejoice together (v. 26). So given the context of the whole chapter, Paul is saying in verse 13 that our baptism unites us to the body of Christ—that is, to a local body of Christ. Baptism inserts you into the living organism that is a local church.

In baptism, two parties speak, and two parties commit. In baptism, you ask for welcome, and the church extends it. In baptism, you pledge yourself to the church, and the church pledges itself to you. The Christian life is not meant to be lived in private, nor is it meant to be lived alone. Baptism brings your life into the light of the church's loving concern. Baptism sets you within the strengthening and sustaining communion of Christ's people.

Three Good Reasons

In this section I've given you three reasons to get baptized. In baptism, (1) you obey Christ's command, (2) you publicly declare your faith in Christ, and (3) you commit to Christ's people. Really, the first reason should suffice. If you're a Christian, obeying what Jesus commands is essential, not optional. And Christ's commands aren't burdensome but liberating and life-giving. His yoke is easy, and his burden is light (Matt. 11:30). When you obey his teaching, you know the truth, and the truth sets you free (John 8:32).

So in addition to simply observing that Christ commands all believers in him to be baptized, we have looked at two aspects of baptism that hold out a blessing for those who do it. In baptism, you declare your faith and thereby exercise and strengthen your faith. In baptism, you commit to Christ's people and thereby inherit the incalculable blessing of local church fellowship.

If you profess faith in Christ, you must be baptized, and being baptized will be a blessing. So what are you waiting for?

I Don't Want to Get Baptized Because . . .

Seriously, what are you waiting for? Why not get baptized as soon as you reasonably can? There are many reasons why professing Christians are reluctant to be baptized as believers. In this section, we'll address seven of the most common reasons people give for not wanting to be baptized.

1. I've Already Been Baptized as an Infant

Maybe you were baptized as an infant. Many Christian traditions practice infant baptism, but they have radically different reasons for doing so. For instance, the Roman Catholic Church teaches that baptism confers saving grace and removes the stain of original sin. That's a drastically different understanding from what I just described above, which means it's a drastically different practice from what most Protestant bodies that practice infant baptism believe.

Among evangelical Christians who practice infant baptism, one of the most common arguments (and, in my opinion, the strongest argument) is offered by Presbyterian and Reformed churches. These churches point out that, in the Old Testament, when God made a covenant with Abraham, he commanded Abraham to apply the sign of the covenant, circumcision, to his (male) children (see Gen. 17:1–14). And God has never explicitly revoked or overturned this pattern of including the children of believers in the covenant community. Therefore, we should apply the sign of the covenant to them. In the new covenant inaugurated by Jesus, the sign of entry is baptism. So, they say, churches today should baptize infants. Such infant baptism is not understood as conferring or guaranteeing salvation. Instead, it is seen as a sign of God's promise.

This argument has much to commend it. I can well understand why believers who are committed to the authority of Scripture would draw this conclusion. But I don't ultimately find it persuasive. Nor do the churches that go by the name of "Baptist," and virtually all non-denominational churches. We can boil down the most decisive reasons against infant baptism into two points.

First, there are no clear instances of infant baptism in the New Testament. Second, every facet of baptism's meaning presupposes the faith of the one being baptized. Jesus commands his disciples to make disciples and to baptize *those disciples* (Matt. 28:19). Baptism is a public profession *of faith* (Acts 2:38–41). In baptism, you commit to Christ and his people—which is something only a believer can and should do (Acts 2:41; 1 Cor. 12:13). Further, baptism symbolizes cleansing (Acts 22:16), death and resurrection with Christ (Rom. 6:1–4), and the regenerating work of the Spirit (Titus 3:5). All of these things are true of those who believe in Christ and only those who believe in Christ.

A second reason why we should reject this rationale for infant baptism is that it misses what's new about the new covenant—the covenant we enjoy through Christ. In Jeremiah 31:31–34, God promises to make a new covenant with his people. This new covenant will not be like the one God made with the people at Mount Sinai, "my covenant that they broke" (v. 32). Instead, "I will put my law within them, and I will write it on their hearts" (v. 33). In the new covenant, the law doesn't stand over God's people as a mere demand but dwells within God's people. In the new covenant, God transforms his people from within, enabling them to desire and do what pleases him. In the new covenant, "they shall all know me, from the least of them to the greatest" (v. 34). Every member of the covenant community will know God personally and intimately. And finally, God gives the ground of this transformed relationship between himself and his people: "For I will forgive their iniquity, and

I will remember their sin no more" (v. 34). To be in the new covenant is to have your sins forgiven through Christ's sacrifice, to know God personally, and to have a transformed heart—a heart on which God's law is now written.

What does all this mean for the Reformed defense of infant baptism? It means that membership in the new covenant comes by new birth not physical birth. It means that by covenantal design, all the members of the new covenant experience the transforming realities of the new covenant. All members of the new covenant know God, have transformed hearts, and have their sins forgiven. There is only one kind of new-covenant member: one who trusts in Christ by the Spirit. The new covenant is made up of believers only, not believers plus their children. If only those who are born again belong to this covenant, then only those who are born again should receive the covenant sign of baptism.

In other words, if you agree with the case I've laid out, then you're compelled to conclude that infant "baptism" is no baptism at all. If baptism is for believers only, and you haven't been baptized as a believer, then you haven't been baptized at all—and you need to be.

2. I Don't Want to Offend My Parents, Who Had Me Baptized as an Infant

This reason is, of course, closely related to the previous one. If your parents had you "baptized" as an infant, and you conclude that wasn't baptism, and you need to be baptized, it's natural to worry whether they will take offense. But should that deter you from getting baptized? Remember that "we will all stand before the judgment seat of God" (Rom. 14:10). Remember that on that day "each will have to bear his own load" (Gal. 6:5). Remember that Jesus claims our absolute loyalty and compels our absolute obedience (Matt. 28:19; Mark 8:34). Normally, obeying Jesus means honoring your parents (Matt. 19:19). But if your parents' desires ever come into conflict with the obedience that Christ commands, Christ's command takes precedence.

So the question is, how should you communicate your new conviction and intent to be baptized to your parents? Do so respectfully and humbly. Express appreciation for the way they raised you in the discipline and nurture of the Lord. Express appreciation for the good intent that motivated them to have you "baptized" as an infant even though you now disagree with the practice. And pray that any disappointment your parents express regarding your different conviction and practice on this point will be easily outweighed by their joy that you are trusting in Christ and seeking to obey him in everything.

3. My Non-Christian Family Will Reject Me

The stakes are much higher here. For many believers around the world today, and even here in the United States, to publicly embrace Christ is to risk being completely cut off by one's natural family. My own church has baptized believers from a variety of religious backgrounds whose families rejected them upon their baptism. This is a great trial and a heavy grief. As church members, we should do all we can to provide for, comfort, and sustain those believers whose obedience to Christ has cost them their families.

We should also remember that this kind of rejection by family is exactly what Jesus said would happen.

> For I have come to set a man against his father, and a daughter against her mother, and a daughter-in-law against her mother-in-law. And a person's enemies will be those of his own household. Whoever loves father or mother more than me is not worthy of me, and whoever loves son or daughter more than me is not worthy of me. (Matt. 10:35–37)

Following Christ is costly, often painfully so. But following Christ is always worth it. Jesus is more than able to repay, both in this life and in the life to come, all that we give up in following him.

> Truly, I say to you, there is no one who has left house or brothers or sisters or mother or father or children or lands, for my sake

and for the gospel, who will not receive a hundredfold now in this time, houses and brothers and sisters and mothers and children and lands, with persecutions, and in the age to come eternal life. (Mark 10:29–30)

If your family is threatening to disown you because you intend to be baptized, I pray that God, by his Spirit, will give you courage to obey this command of Christ. I pray that he will bless your bold obedience and that he will be with you in whatever trials he ordains for you.

4. I'm Afraid to Tell Everyone I'm a Christian

In the West today, the tide of public support for Christianity continues to recede. To be a Christian today is to be more exposed—exposed to ridicule, opposition, disfavor, losing a job. But confessing Christ has always been costly: "For which of you, desiring to build a tower, does not first sit down and count the cost, whether he has enough to complete it?" (Luke 14:28). What cost does Christ require us to pay in order to follow him? "So therefore, any one of you who does not renounce all that he has cannot be my disciple" (v. 33). "All that he has" certainly includes reputation, favor, and career.

If you're afraid to publicly declare yourself a Christian, you should recognize this as one of the first temptations you will face. If the prospect of baptism is testing your faith, then it's just the test you need. Will you pass it? Consider Jesus's somber warning: "So everyone who acknowledges me before men, I also will acknowledge before my Father who is in heaven, but whoever denies me before men, I also will deny before my Father who is in heaven" (Matt. 10:32–33).

5. I'm Afraid of Speaking in Public

Some people fear baptism because they're afraid of speaking in public. For instance, at my church, the process of being baptized goes like this: A new believer takes our membership class, has an interview with a pastor, and is then approved by the elders and the congregation. During the Sunday morning service on which they're baptized, we ask them to share with the congregation, in about three minutes, how the Lord brought them to faith in Christ. These are tremendously encouraging times. The congregation typically erupts in joyful clapping after each testimony. But for a variety of reasons, not everyone is either able or comfortable making this brief speech. In those rare cases, we are happy for that person simply to answer two questions in the affirmative that we always publicly ask baptismal candidates: "Do you make profession of repentance toward God and of faith in the Lord Jesus Christ?" and "Do you promise, by God's grace, to follow him forever in the fellowship of his church?"

If the normal practice at your church is for baptismal candidates to share their testimonies, and if for any reason that is a serious difficulty for you, ask your pastors if they offer a similar accommodation. Baptism requires that you publicly declare your faith in Christ. How many words you use is far less important.

6. I've Been a Believer for a Long Time. Isn't It Too Late?

What if you've been a believer for a long time? Perhaps you've taken a long time pondering the validity of your infant "baptism." Perhaps you simply never got around to being baptized. In any case, it has been years or even decades since you became a Christian. And isn't baptism supposed to happen right after conversion? Doesn't that mean it's too late now?

Yes, you are supposed to get baptized right after you come to faith. But no, that doesn't mean it's too late now. Jesus's command to be baptized is binding on all believers, which means it is binding on you. Whatever your reasons for not yet obeying Christ's command, none of those are good reasons for now refusing to be baptized.

Jesus once told a parable of a man who had two sons. He told the first son to go work in his vineyard, and the son first answered "I will not," but later "he changed his mind and went" (Matt. 21:28–29). When the man did the same with his other son, the second son said he would go but didn't (v. 30). Then Jesus asked, "Which of the two did the will of his father?" (v. 31). The answer is obvious: the first. In context, Jesus's point was that many who were obviously sinners, but who realized it and repented, were entering the kingdom ahead of those who were rejecting Jesus (v. 31). But his principle extends to baptism too. When it comes to any of Christ's commands, baptism included, late is better than never.

7. I Don't Want to Join a Church

Some who profess faith in Christ may be willing to get baptized but not willing to join a church. To them, church membership sounds too much like organized religion: too formal or too authoritarian. Now, some churches baptize people without breathing a word about church membership. However well-intentioned, such churches are doing believers a disservice and are pulling apart what the Bible keeps together. Remember what we saw when we considered Acts 2:38–41 and 1 Corinthians 12:13? In baptism, you not only commit to Christ, you commit to Christ's people. And church membership simply is the committed relationship between a church and a Christian that baptism begins.

But maybe you still have lingering doubts about church membership. Maybe you're not convinced that the relationship between a Christian and a local church needs to take such a committed, accountable shape. If that's you, I want to persuade you that church membership is biblical and that it's basic to the Christian life.

Let's start with a little more detailed definition: Church membership is a mutual, self-conscious commitment between a church and a Christian in which the church affirms and cares for the Christian, and the Christian submits to and cares for the church.

There are three biblical pillars that support this understanding of church membership. The first is that, throughout the New Testament, the church has a clearly defined "inside" and "outside." In Matthew 18:17, Jesus commands us to notify "the church" of a brother or sister's unrepentant sin, and he commands "the church" to remove that person from its fellowship if there is no repentance. Who is to be notified? Who is to act? This can only be a body of people who have willingly and knowingly assumed accountability for one another and submitted themselves to each other.

Further, in a similar scenario, the apostle Paul instructs the church in Corinth to remove from its fellowship someone who was committing unrepentant sexual sin (1 Cor 5:1–13). He writes, "For what have I to do with judging outsiders? Is it not those inside the church whom you are to judge?" (v. 12). Note the opposite treatment Paul prescribes depending on whether someone is outside or inside the church. We are to expect that outsiders, those who do not profess faith in Christ, will live as non-Christians, so we are not to separate ourselves from them in response to their sin. On the other hand, we *are* to withdraw fellowship from those who are "inside" the church— those who profess faith in Christ but whose lives contradict that profession. You can only be put *out* if you were first put *in*. The church only has the authority to "judge" those who have consciously committed themselves to the church's authority.

A second biblical support for church membership is the wide range of metaphors in the New Testament that portray believers as bound together, knit together, stuck together into the shape of a local church. We are members of God's household (1 Tim. 3:15). We are stones in God's temple (Eph. 2:21–22). We are members of Christ's body (1 Cor. 12:12–26). In each case, whatever those images may imply about our belonging to the universal body of Christ, those images all imply and require real relationships with real people who are really known by and committed to each other.

Third, all the New Testament's commands about how we should live together as believers presuppose this commitment to a body of believers. For instance, in Ephesians 4:15–16, we are told to speak the truth in love to each other, so that we grow up into Christ, which happens "when each part is working properly." How can we know whether each part of the

body is working properly if we don't know who
the parts are? How can the parts of the body
help each other grow if they aren't joined together in a vital, organic, mutually dependent
relationship?

So instead of refusing baptism because you
don't want to join a church, I would encourage
you—exhort you, even—to be baptized precisely
so that you *can* join a church. Church membership is a practical foundation for the entire
Christian life. It's not an optional add-on for elite
believers but a help and support and means of
grace for all believers.

But What About . . . ?

If you still have unanswered questions and objections about baptism, I'd encourage you to
pray about them, search Scripture for answers to
them, and discuss them with a pastor or another
mature Christian you trust.

But assuming you're convinced you need to
be baptized, what should you do now? Good
question. That brings us to our last section.

What Should I Do Now?

What should you do now? I've got a one-sentence encouragement for you: Find a church that preaches the gospel and pursue baptism as part of joining the church. Let's unpack this statement in four parts.

Find a Church . . .

First, find a church. Maybe one of the reasons you haven't been baptized is that your church attendance has been selective and spotty. It's time to reverse that trend. Find a church you can regularly attend and commit to the church. Show up every Sunday. Get to know people. Get to know the church's pastors. Let them know you want to be baptized and follow through on the steps they give you.[2]

. . . That Preaches the Gospel . . .

The most important thing about a church is that it preaches the gospel. Sadly, not every church does. Some so-called churches deny

Jesus's atoning death and bodily resurrection. Some so-called churches do not agree with the Bible that we are justified (declared righteous by God) by his grace alone through faith alone in Christ alone. Instead, such so-called churches teach that we are made right with God by "faith plus x"—such as "faith plus our good works," which ultimately make us acceptable to God. Shun all such assemblies.

Some churches affirm the gospel but generally assume the gospel. If you poke the right places, the gospel will spring out, but the church doesn't regularly proclaim the gospel. Before settling at a church like this, I would encourage you to search diligently, within as wide an area as you can reasonably canvass, for a church that delights to put the gospel front and center in all it does.

So, instead of a church that denies or assumes the gospel, you want to attend, join, and get baptized by a church that preaches the gospel, celebrates the gospel, and promotes the gospel. You want to join a church whose weekly worship will strengthen your grip on the gospel and help you not forget the gospel.

. . . And Pursue Baptism . . .

Once you've settled on a gospel-preaching church to join, pursue baptism. Talk to a pastor. Find out what next steps they want you to take and take them. Baptism won't pursue you; you have to pursue it.

. . . As Part of Joining the Church

As we discussed in the last chapter, not every church requires those being baptized to pursue membership at the same time. I've tried to show why this is a mistake. But even if your church happens to leave that door open to you, I would encourage you not to go through it. Instead, follow all the way through on what Scripture says that baptism is and does. If you trust in Christ, then get baptized in order to obey Christ's command to publicly profess your faith in Christ and to commit to Christ and his people.

Notes

1. Bobby Jamieson, *Understanding Baptism*, Church Basics (Nashville, TN: B&H, 2016), 6.
2. If you need help finding a church, you might start with the 9Marks church search, at www.9marks.org /church-search/.

Recommended Resources

Bobby Jamieson. *Going Public: Why Baptism Is Required for Church Membership*. Nashville, TN: B&H, 2015.

Bobby Jamieson. *Understanding Baptism*. Church Basics. Nashville, TN: B&H, 2016.

Scripture Index

IX 9Marks

Building Healthy Churches

9Marks exists to equip church leaders with a biblical vision and practical resources for displaying God's glory to the nations through healthy churches.

To that end, we want to see churches characterized by these nine marks of health:

1. Expositional Preaching
2. Gospel Doctrine
3. A Biblical Understanding of Conversion and Evangelism
4. Biblical Church Membership
5. Biblical Church Discipline
6. A Biblical Concern for Discipleship and Growth
7. Biblical Church Leadership
8. A Biblical Understanding of the Practice of Prayer
9. A Biblical Understanding and Practice of Missions

Find all our Crossway titles and other resources at 9Marks.org.

John Onwuchekwa
Church Questions

Sam Emadi
Church Questions

Mark Dever
Church Questions

I Like Church?

Does God Love Everyone?
Matt McCullough
Church Questions

How Can I Find Someone to Disciple Me?
J. Garrett Kell
Church Questions

How Can Women T the Local
Keri Folmar
Church Questions

How Can Our Church Find a Faithful Pastor?
Mark Dever
Church Questions

Is It Loving to Practice Church Discipline?
Jonathan Leeman
Church Questions

How Can I Love Ch Members Different
Jonathan & Andy N
Church Questions

IX 9Marks Church Questions

Providing ordinary Christians with sound and
accessible biblical teaching by answering
common questions about church life.

For more information, visit crossway.org.